BIBLE NEWS PROPHECY

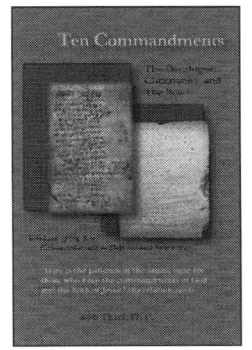 8
 16
 28

In This Issue:

2 **From the Editor: The Feast of Trumpets and Jesus' Return** Should Christians keep the Feast of Trumpets?

4 **Christ Said - WATCH!** What should we watch? Will all in the Philadelphia remnant be protected?

8 **The Fourth Commandment** Is it still in effect?

16 **Study the Bible Course Lesson 16a: You Must Be Born Again!** How and when?

27 **Exercise! Who Needs It?** Should you exercise?

28 **Youth and Singles Q&A** This article answers questions some teens and singles have wondered about.

Back Cover: Internet and Radio This shows where people can find the messages from the *Continuing* Church of God.

About the Front Cover: Thousands of years ago, the children of Israel crossed the Red Sea on the 7th Day of Unleavened Bread. May there be ramifications in the 21st century? Cover developed for the Continuing Church of God.

Bible News Prophecy magazine is published by the *Continuing* Church of God, 1036 W. Grand Avenue, Grover Beach, CA, 93433. http://www.ccog.org

©2019 *Continuing* Church of God. Printed in the U.S.A. All rights reserved.

Reproduction in whole or in part without written permission is prohibited. We do respect your privacy and we do not rent, trade, or sell our mailing list. If you do not want to receive this magazine, simply contact our Grover Beach office. Scripture references are from the New King James Version (©Thomas Nelson, Inc., Publishers, used by permission or for 20th century articles the KJV) unless otherwise noted.

Bible News Prophecy – SUPPORTED BY YOUR CONTRIBUTIONS

Bible News Prophecy has no subscription or newsstand price. This magazine is provided free of charge by the Continuing Church of God. It is made possible by the voluntary, freely given tithes and offerings of the membership of the Church and others who have elected to support the work of the Church. Contributions are gratefully welcomed and are tax-deductible in the U.S. Those who wish to voluntarily aid and support this worldwide Work of God are gladly welcomed as co-workers in this major effort to preach and publish the gospel to all nations. Contributions should be sent to: Continuing Church of God, 1036 W. Grand Avenue, Grover Beach, CA, 93433.

Editor in Chief: Bob Thiel

Copy/Proofing Editor: Joyce Thiel

Proofreader: John Hickey;
SBC Course Assister: Shirley Gestro.

Photos: All photos come from the Thiel family or public domain sources such as Wikipedia, Pixabay, or certain governments (unless specific attribution is given).

Layout and Design:
James Erwin Estoque

July – September 2019

FROM THE EDITOR IN CHIEF: BOB THIEL

THE FEAST OF TRUMPETS AND JESUS' RETURN

Most of the Greco-Roman churches do not keep the biblical holy days that generally occur in the Fall. Yet, these Holy Days portray many pivotal events in God's plan.

The Feast of Trumpets not only pictures the coming of Christ to resurrect the firstfruits from the dead, it also pictures the terrible time of devastation just ahead and the intervention of Jesus Christ to save the living from total annihilation and to establish the Kingdom of God on earth.

Let's understand how this festival fits into God's great master plan.

Consider that there is a major time gap between the Day of Pentecost and the Feast of Trumpets. Since the New Testament church began on Pentecost and basically ends when Jesus returns at the last trumpet (1 Corinthians 15:51-57), in a sense the period of time between Pentecost and the Feast of Trumpets can be considered as representing the church age.

The fourth Holy Day, the Feast of Trumpets, is observed in "the seventh month, on the first day of the month" (Leviticus 23:23-25).

The number seven in God's plan signifies completion and perfection. The seventh month of God's calendar (occurs in September and/or October) contains the final four festivals, picturing the completion of God's great master plan for us. The festival that falls on the first day of this month marks the beginning of the final events in God's plan.

It is another annual Sabbath of rest from one's regular work, and it was to be a memorial of blowing of trumpets (Leviticus 23:24-25). It is also a time to learn God's ways (Nehemiah 8:2-3; cf. Ezra 3:1-7). Much of what happened to the children of Israel was written for our "examples, and they were written for our admonition, upon whom the ends of the ages have come" (1 Corinthians 10:11).

It is from the blowing of trumpets that the Feast of Trumpets draws its name.

There is a great deal of symbolic meaning tied in with the blowing of these trumpets, especially with regard to the end times in which we're living. It should be noted that the modern Jewish name for this date, Rosh Hashanah, is not biblical nor even original for the Jews. It was something that they adopted centuries after God gave it to them and after the Old Testament was written (Kramer, Amy J. Rosh Hashana Origins. Copyright © 1998-1999 Everything Jewish, Inc.).

The Bible teaches that Trumpets were blown to announce God's feasts, as well as to call people to assemble (Numbers 10:1-3, 10).

Book of Life

Interestingly, Jewish scholars have tied the Feast of Trumpets in with the 'Book of Life' (Peltz M, Rabbi. What is in a Rosh Hashanah greeting? Haaretz, September 17, 2012). Why is that of interest?

Well, the Bible teaches that those who are listed in the 'Book of Life' (Philippians 4:3; Revelation 3:5) will be resurrected (Hebrews 12:22-23). When? At the seventh and last trumpet:

> 51 Behold, I tell you a mystery: We shall not all sleep, but we shall all be changed — 52 in a moment, in the twinkling of an eye, at the last trumpet. For the trumpet will sound, and the dead will be raised incorruptible, and we shall be changed. 53 For this corruptible must put on incorruption, and this mortal must put on immortality. (1 Corinthians 15:51-53)

The Book of Revelation clearly teaches that seven trumpets will be blown (8:2), punishment comes upon those who are not protected by God (9:4), and then God's kingdom and judgment will come (11:15-18).

Finally it teaches that those whose names are not written in the Book of Life will experience the second death (Revelation 20:14-15).

Trumpet Blasts

Consider that the Bible shows that during Israel's history, which was heavily punctuated with conflicts and rebellion, trumpets continued to be used as warning devices, to call to arms or as preludes to important messages — always to mark an event of tremendous import to the whole nation.

God also used the prophets, among them Isaiah, Ezekiel, Hosea and Joel, to warn Israel about punishments He would bring upon them for their constant rebellion against His laws. These prophets were to use their voices like trumpets to blare their warnings to God's people.

> 1 Cry aloud, spare not; Lift up your voice like a trumpet; Tell My people their transgression, And the house of Jacob their sins. (Isaiah 58:1)

We in the Continuing Church of God are working to do that today. We boldly tell of the sins of society and how world events are aligning with properly understood prophecy--which we also strive to explain.

But there will also be literal trumpet blasts coming in the future as the Book of Revelation teaches (Revelation 8:1-13, 9:1-18). But most will not heed those warnings.

Many are blown in the Book of Revelation, and a lot were to be blown on the Feast of Trumpets (Leviticus 23:24)--hopefully many can see the connection.

But the most important trumpet, in a sense, could be the last, the seventh one. Here is what Revelation teaches about that:

> 15 Then the seventh angel sounded: And there were loud voices in heaven, saying, "The kingdoms of this world have become the kingdoms of our Lord and of His Christ, and He shall reign forever and ever!" 16 And the twenty-four elders who sat before God on their thrones fell on their faces and worshiped God, 17 saying: "We give You thanks, O Lord God Almighty, The One who is and who was and who is to come, Because You have taken Your great power and reigned. 18 The nations were angry, and Your wrath has come, And the time of the dead, that they should be judged, And that You should reward Your servants the prophets and the saints, And those who fear Your name, small and great, And should destroy those who destroy the earth." 19 Then the temple of God was opened in heaven, and the ark of His covenant was seen in His temple. And there were lightnings, noises, thunderings, an earthquake, and great hail. (Revelation 11:15-19)

The Feast of Trumpets pictures the future blowing of trumpets and the reality that Jesus will come and establish the Kingdom of God on the earth. The good news of coming Kingdom of God is a big part of what Jesus wants His servants to proclaim now (Matthew 24:14; 28:19-20) and then the end will come (Matthew 24:14). The Feast of Trumpets points to Christ's victory over this world.

Greco-Roman historians, such as Jerome and Epiphanius (Catholica Omnia Tabulinum De Ecclesiae Patribus Doctoribusque Materia Migne JP Argumentum Patrologia Latina Volumen MPL025 Ab Columna ad Culumnam 1415 - 1542A, pp. 922, 930 and Epiphanius (Ephiphanius. The Panarion of Ephiphanius of Salamis: Bock II (sects 1-46) Section 1, Chapter 19, 7-9. Frank Williams, editor. Publisher BRILL, 1987, p. 117-119)), recorded that the 'Nazarene Christians' continued to keep the Fall Holy Days into the fourth and fifth centuries. They were also kept by the faithful Christians in Jerusalem who claimed the original Christian building in Jerusalem into the fourth century until they were stopped by Imperial authorities (Pixner B. Church of the Apostles Found on Mt. Zion. Biblical Archaeology Review, May/June 1990: 16-35,60).

The anti-Semite John Chrysostom specifically attempted to stop people from keeping the Feast of Trumpets in the late fourth century (John Chrysostom. Homily I Against the Jews I:5;VI:5;VII:2). However, those trying to be faithful continued to do so throughout history. The Continuing Church of God does so now.

In 2019, the Feast of Trumpets begins at sunset September 29th and runs through sunset September 30th.

Christ Said - WATCH!

By Charles Hunting

This article contains excerpts from an article published in the September 1967 Good News magazine.

What did Christ mean? You may not know the answer. Your future safety will depend on HOW you watch! Learn to avoid the tragedy of USELESS watching. ...

I wondered how many people in God's Church are taking the warning to run for our lives.

Notice! I said are taking, not will take. Realize it or not, our flight has ALREADY BEGUN! We already face much greater peril than any of these refugees. Don't harbor the delusion that this flight is merely going to be a call at some specified date, that as long as you keep the lines of communication open between yourself and the Church you will pack and leave.

Don't get the idea that because we may be "cast out" we will be part of that group. It would be real simple, wouldn't it, to harbor the idea that because some government, in anger, casts out the Church, the flight will be obvious. You are a part of the Church — you may reason — hence you will be cast out and go to a place of safety with the {remnant of the} Philadelphia Church.

If you ride this delusion you are going to take a swift ride into the tribulation — and I CAN PROVE IT!

Let's face reality! God does not warn in vain. He does not need to fill up space — to pad out a story. Every word written in His Book is written out of love and concern FOR us!

God said He is going to pour out His Spirit on us and make His words KNOWN to us! But He also warns that when He does this, people will not turn at His reproof.

And, tragically, because we refuse to heed, God is going to totally disregard us when panic, distress and anguish come upon us! (Prov. 1:23-28.)

We do KNOW for sure that over two million people are going to be told to flee — but won't!

Judah Will Not Flee

Let me explain.

Judah ... WILL NOT LISTEN.

> "Run ye to and fro through the streets of Jerusalem, and see now, and know, and seek in the broad places thereof, if ye can find a man, if there be any that executes judgment, that seeks the truth; and I will pardon it. And though they say, The Lord lives; surely they swear falsely.... you have stricken them, but they have not grieved; you have consumed them, but they have refused to receive correction: they have made their faces harder than a rock; they have REFUSED TO RETURN! (Jer. 5:1-3.)

Read Matthew 24:16.

> "Then let them which be in Judaea FLEE into the mountains."

Get a map of Israel and Jordan. Look HOW CLOSE they are to a place called Petra — a possible place of safety. That's pretty close, isn't it? It's a thirty-minute plane ride — a four-hour automobile ride.

Isn't it just a little sad that the people physically closest to the place of safety will probably be less likely to take the opportunity?

Let's look at the rest of Israel. What is prophesied for the United States and Great Britain staggers the imagination and defies description.

Do words like United States and Great Britain seem impersonal to you? All right, let's make it personal. Your state, your county, city or town — perhaps your own relatives — and maybe YOU are going to know terror which has never yet been described or experienced!

You think that is a sensational statement that can't be

backed up? Well, let me tell you, it isn't!

Jeremiah cried out in horror when he saw the future of those two great nations.

> "ALAS! for that day is GREAT, so that NONE is like it: it is even the time of Jacob's {Ephraim and Manasseh's) trouble" (Jer. 30:7).

Coming — Time of Terror

Don't carelessly gloss over what it says! It plainly says no time of suffering or horror has EVER approached this time!

These days have no parallel in ALL history. No horror stories yet written of the bestiality, savagery and atrocities of the Nazi concentration camps are capable of showing the misery to come! There has NEVER been a time like it!

And here is the warning for the Church!

Notice! "And some of those who are wise SHALL FALL" — for what purpose? — "to refine and cleanse them…" (Dan. 11:35).

God is going to literally haul Israel into total destruction. But of all the people of Israel those in God's Church have the matchless gift of being called — not just to survival in horror — but to survival in safety (Rev. 12:14).

Unbelievably, some won't choose this way. They will do it the hard way. God specifically says of some,

> "Take from these [those who are going to die or be taken captive] a small number and bind them in the skirts of your robes. And of these [those offered a place of safety], take of them again, and cast them into the midst of the fire, and burn them in the fire…" (Ezek. 5:3-4).

Ezekiel could be talking about some of us! Does it disturb you to know that there are specific prophecies about some of us?

The big question is, WHY? Why, with all the fantastic warnings we have been exposed to, should it happen to any of us? We have had some startling prophecies fulfilled right before our eyes in the last few months.

… there should be a DEEP REALIZATION that what Ezekiel said about those who could have been saved but were cast into the fire WILL TAKE PLACE.

Don't let this be a prophecy about YOU!

We Can Know the Future

Let's understand, brethren, our minds have been opened. We KNOW God! Israel and the rest of the world is going to know God through great tribulation.

> "So will I stretch out my hand upon them, and make the land desolate, yea, more desolate than the wilderness toward Diblath, in ALL THEIR HABITATIONS: and they SHALL KNOW that I am the Lord" (Ezek. 6:14).

These are stern warnings …

Why have we been given knowledge of these prophecies? It is because they are the warning signs to members of God's Church who have a mind to see that we are approaching the end of the road. Just as surely as the diminishing mileage pictured on road signs as you draw closer to your destination, these prophecies are our road signs — our mileage markers!

Are we blind to them? Do they have a profound affect upon us? If they don't, there is a specific reason and that reason is terribly important.

The only reason we see or can see is because we have something to spotlight the danger in our minds. The world CAN'T SEE. Just like a darkened road sign at night without some illumination the world can't see the signpost.

The world can see something is wrong, but blindly continues on the path of destruction because it knows no other path. They will hear the broadcast, they hear the prophecies, and see the fulfillment. But there is no real sense of danger.

What Does It Mean to "Watch"?

Let me explain it to you this way. You and I are just as interested today as we were yesterday in preserving our physical lives. If we saw physical danger approaching we would react just as fast as our ability would permit. We watch alertly for approaching danger when driving an automobile. If danger approaches, we take every precaution possible to preserve our lives — just like the American refugees fleeing the Arabs.

There is a big danger, however. We think we will be aware and be watching for the danger that is to come upon our people. And we will if we know what it means to watch. But we must understand the Biblical meaning of watching. There is a vast difference between watching God's way and watching the world's way!

Let's assume you watched as the governments of this world do. They spend millions on watching. Huge espionage rings and fantastic communication facilities with listening posts around the world to spot danger by the mode of the day. In every intelligible language, skilled men analyze newspapers, magazines, books and periodicals written in foreign languages. Learned men spend lifetimes in learning languages and how to analyze the slightest movement of a foreign power.

Governments watch with physical resources. The United States has spent literally billions on earth satellites to keep track of the weather. They know what it is worldwide.

Now, let me ask you this question — what good does it do? At best there is a possibility that they can warn some few people to move out of a possible storm area or international trouble spot. But they don't have the power to watch in the way that could or will save their lives … (Amos 9:1-4).

Do the Right Kind of Watching

Only we are given the power to escape! What did Christ mean then when He said to watch and pray always, that we may be accounted worthy to escape? (Luke 21:36.)

He didn't mean it the way the Pharisees watched. They watched Christ — selfishly — for their own personal gain (Luke 14:1). Christ didn't tell us to watch for the purpose of escape. That would only serve a selfish purpose.

The word "watching" indicates a person has a sense of danger. Watching is a job. We are called His watchmen (Ezek. 33:1-9). A watchman is alert and aware of what is going on. He usually watches at a time of darkness because that is the time of greatest danger.

Christ said, watch and pray that you might be worthy to escape. All right, you just get down on your knees right now and ask God, "Please help me to be worthy to escape." Will that prayer make you more worthy to escape than you were when you went down on your knees? I doubt it seriously!

The watching and praying, brethren, is not a watching and praying for ourselves to escape. The watching and praying is what is done by an individual who is in the process of becoming worthy. By offering a prayer that we might be worthy, does it make us worthy? No! Of course not!

If we are only praying to escape, these prophecies will have little meaning!

Do YOU understand this? Or are we in the condition of the world — hearing and yet not perceiving? God doesn't want it this way. It is our doing. God gave His Spirit that we might understand.

That is why Christ said, Watch! "Watch therefore: for you know not what hour [there is some uncertainty] your Lord does come" (Mat. 24:42). It is called a time of great darkness.

The only ones who can watch in the way Christ intended (to become worthy to escape) are the people who are not in darkness.

Are You Worthy to Escape?

There are going to be millions who know through the broadcast and The PLAIN TRUTH what is going to take place but who are not going to be accounted worthy to escape!

Many are going to "almost" make it!

They are going to be, OH SO CLOSE. Just as close as their radio. Some are going to be ever so much closer. They are going to be in the very company of those who will make it. Notice Daniel: "But many shall cleave to them with flatteries. And some of them of understanding shall fall, to try them, and to purge, and to make them white…" (Dan. 11:34, 35). That's real close. Close enough not to have missed.

But then look at the Ten Virgins. You can't get any

closer than they were. Notice Matthew 25:6, "And at midnight (a period of great darkness) there was a cry made..." There is a great cry going out in this period of great spiritual darkness. In this hour of great darkness there is light. That is, for those who want it. This parable shows clearly that the wise took "oil." Because they "took" the oil (did what was necessary to acquire the ingredients that would light their path) they could see at a time of darkness.

Without oil they couldn't see. Neither can we! These tremendous warnings, the unbelievable opening of prophecy to God's servants, will not be plain and clear OR motivate you unless they are spotlighted by the illumination of God's Holy Spirit.

Don't be like the Foolish Virgins. They saw it too late — just when the rest of the world did.

They saw danger, but the curtain had dropped — it was too late!

I have seen just how fast the borders can be closed. I was about to participate in the most exciting phase of God's Work in 1,900 years, and WHAM! the door was closed. Doors are going to be closed even more swiftly in the future. A blitzkrieg attack could close off any part of the world and its borders in minutes — especially in the Middle East.

Be Spiritually Motivated

What we must come to understand is that the flight is physical. But it's going to be SPIRITUALLY MOTIVATED. Without seeing in the light of God's Spirit we are like those described in Matthew 13: "And in them is fulfilled the prophecy of Isaiah, which says, By hearing you shall hear, and shall not understand; and seeing you shall see, and not perceive: For this people's heart is waxed gross, and their ears are dull of hearing, and their eyes THEY HAVE CLOSED..." (verses 14-15).

Yes, I know this refers to the world. But it also refers to ANYONE who permits his eyes (spiritually speaking) to close.

Yes, we should watch, but watch in a particular way. You could subscribe to all leading newspapers, periodicals, magazines and study them diligently {or in this century, study news articles on the internet}. You can listen to news on the radio and television. Yes, you might even read The PLAIN TRUTH {or Bible News Prophecy} magazine and study it until your eyeballs become bloodshot and hang to your knees — and still miss the boat! That's what the world is doing.

Here is how we are to watch. The Holy Spirit inspired Peter to write, "The end of all things is at hand: be you therefore sober, and WATCH UNTO PRAYER" (I Peter 4:7).

This is the key to the WAY we should watch. This is how the prophetic knowledge will cause us to react so we can become worthy. This is how we will really understand. This is the big test!

If these prophecies are a reality in our mind we will be engaging in more of the spiritual work of God's Church — praying! fasting! serving the brethren!

Be Spiritually Alive

Notice carefully in Luke 21 the admonition: "And TAKE HEED to yourselves [carefully examine yourself], lest at any time your hearts be overcharged with surfeiting [the opposite of fasting], and drunkenness, and cares of this life..." (verse 34). Making the cares of this life your first concern is going to take you in exactly the opposite direction from concern for God's Work. God's Work will lose meaning for you! You will no longer care about the broadcast in England, or any part of God's Work around the world. And if this is true, brethren, this day will come "as a snare to those who dwell on the face of the whole earth" (verse 35).

The word "watch" means to become spiritually alive — spiritually active! This isn't {just} a matter of seeing with our eyes. It is not a matter of looking at newspapers or a magazine, or hearing a broadcast, or even reading The PLAIN TRUTH. You could be blind and deaf and still do God's Work. This is a matter of a spiritually active individual!

Let's ask ourselves, brethren, if we are spiritually alive. Are we watching in the right way? If we are, we are putting out ALL effort in this last-ditch struggle to get the Work of God done.

Brethren, let's examine ourselves so we won't just almost make the really BIG EVENTS to follow! WATCH GOD'S WAY!

Editor: Many in the world, as well as many Laodiceans, are watching events and hoping that doing so will save them. While Jesus told His followers to watch, He also warned:

> *25 For whoever desires to save his life will lose it, but whoever loses his life for My sake will find it. 26 For what profit is it to a man if he gains the whole world, and loses his own soul? Or what will a man give in exchange for his soul? 27 For the Son of Man will come in the glory of His Father with His angels, and then He will reward each according to his works. (Matthew 16:25-27)*

So, watching involves more than just seeing events to try to save ones life. Christ's followers need to lose their lives for His sake. Yet that is NOT a statement about martyrdom (though that will happen to some), but an admonition to not live according to your own ways and will, but fully to live according to God's way and will.

The FOURTH Commandment

By Bob Thiel

Our lives are often busy.

We need to become educated (at least informally), make a living, take care of our families, etc. There are also numerous distractions and various ones who want to impose on our time.

Do humans need a rest from the world of today?

The Book of Genesis teaches the following:

> 1 Thus the heavens and the earth, and all the host of them, were finished. 2 And on the seventh day God ended His work which He had done, and He rested on the seventh day from all His work which He had done. 3 Then God blessed the seventh day and sanctified it, because in it He rested from all His work which God had created and made. (Genesis 2:1-3)

Is the Sabbath still needed and valid for today?

Who did Jesus say God made the Sabbath for?

> 27 "The Sabbath was made for man, and not man for the Sabbath. 28 Therefore the Son of Man is also Lord of the Sabbath." (Mark 2:27-28)

Some, including those calling themselves Jehovah's Witnesses, have claimed that God made the Sabbath for Himself in Genesis 2 and that He then gave it to the Jews over 2500 years later.

But Jesus said the Sabbath was made for man, meaning all humans and not just Jews. Furthermore, although many want to call Sunday 'The Lord's Day,' in the Bible, Jesus said He was Lord of the Sabbath.

In the English language, the seventh-day of the week is called Saturday. Yet, most who profess Christianity either do not believe it needs to be kept at all or believe to some degree it is to be kept on Sunday.

But the Bible never teaches that.

The fourth commandment from the Book of Exodus is listed as follows:

> 8 "Remember the Sabbath day, to keep it holy. 9 Six days you shall labor and do all your work, 10 but the seventh day is the Sabbath of the Lord your God. In it you shall do no work: you, nor your son, nor your daughter, nor your male servant, nor your female servant, nor your cattle, nor your stranger who is within your gates. 11 For in six days the Lord made the heavens and the earth, the sea, and all that is in them, and rested

the seventh day. Therefore the Lord blessed the Sabbath day and hallowed it. (Exodus 20:8-11)

People should work when they need to and rest on the Sabbath. This author has long considered the Sabbath to be a paid vacation. It is paid by working throughout the week, and since it is a command of God, one can be confident that God will provide when you take that one day per week off.

Christians are to Observe the Seventh Day Sabbath

Many oppose the Sabbath. Some have even argued that the New Testament does not enjoin the seventh-day Sabbath, but that is an erroneous belief.
Jesus taught:

> 4 "It is written, 'Man shall not live by bread alone, but by every word that proceeds from the mouth of God.'" (Matthew 4:4)

The Apostle Paul taught:

> 16 All Scripture is given by inspiration of God, and is profitable for doctrine, for reproof, for correction, for instruction in righteousness, 17 that the man of God may be complete, thoroughly equipped for every good work. (2 Timothy 3:16-17)

So, does the portion of scripture known as the New Testament enjoin keeping the Sabbath for Christians? Notice what the New Testament Book of Hebrews teaches using two Protestant and three Catholic translations:

> 3 Now we who have believed enter that rest, just as God has said, "So I declared on oath in my anger, 'They shall never enter my rest.'" And yet his work has been finished since the creation of the world. 4 For somewhere he has spoken about the seventh day in these words: "And on the seventh day God rested from all his work." 5 And again in the passage above he says, "They shall never enter my rest." 6 It still remains that some will enter that rest, and those who formerly had the gospel preached to them did not go in, because of their disobedience...9 There remains, then, a Sabbath-rest for the people of God; 10 for anyone who enters God's rest also rests from his own work, just as God did from his. 11 Let us, therefore, make every effort to enter that rest, so that no one will fall by following their example of disobedience (Hebrews 4:3-6,9-11, NIV).

> 3 For we who have believed enter that rest, just as He has said, "AS I SWORE IN MY WRATH, THEY SHALL NOT ENTER MY REST," although His works were finished from the foundation of the world. 4 For He has said somewhere concerning the seventh day: "AND GOD RESTED ON THE SEVENTH DAY FROM ALL HIS WORKS"; 5 and again in this passage, "THEY SHALL NOT ENTER MY REST." 6 Therefore, since it remains for some to enter it, and those who formerly had good news preached to them failed to enter because of disobedience,.. 9 So there remains a Sabbath rest for the people of God. 10 For the one who has entered His rest has himself also rested from his works, as God did from His. 11 Therefore let us be diligent to enter that rest, so that no one will fall, through following the same example of disobedience. (Hebrews 4:3-6,9-11, NASB)

> 3 We, however, who have faith, are entering a place of rest, as in the text: And then in my anger I swore that they would never enter my place of rest. Now God's work was all finished at the beginning of the world; 4 as one text says, referring to the seventh day: And God rested on the seventh day after all the work he had been doing. 5 And, again, the passage above says: They will never reach my place of rest. 6 It remains the case, then, that there would be some people who would reach it, and since those who first heard the good news were prevented from entering by their refusal to believe...9 There must still be, therefore, a seventh-day rest reserved for God's people, 10 since to enter the place of rest is to rest after your work, as God did after his. 11 Let us, then, press forward to enter this place of rest, or some of you might copy this example of refusal to believe and be lost. (Hebrews 4:3-6,9-11, NJB)

3 For we, that have believed, shall enter into their rest; as he said: As I sware in my wrath, if they shall enter into my rest: and truly the works from the foundation of the world being perfected. 4 For he said in a certain place of the seventh day thus: And God rested the seventh day from all his works...9 Therefore there is left a sabbatisme for the people of God. 10 For he that is entered into his rest, the same also hath rested from his works, as God did from his. 11 Let us hasten therefore to enter into that rest; lest any man fall into the same example of incredulity. (Hebrews 4:3-6,9-11, The Original and True Rheims New Testament of Anno Domini 1582)

3 For we who believed enter into [that] rest, just as he has said: "As I swore in my wrath, 'They shall not enter into my rest,'" and yet his works were accomplished at the foundation of the world. 4 For he has spoken somewhere about the seventh day in this manner, "And God rested on the seventh day from all his works"; 5 and again, in the previously mentioned place, "They shall not enter into my rest." 6 Therefore, since it remains that some will enter into it, and those who formerly received the good news did not enter because of disobedience,... 9 Therefore, a sabbath rest still remains for the people of God. 10 And whoever enters into God's rest, rests from his own works as God did from his. 11 Therefore, let us strive to enter into that rest, so that no one may fall after the same example of disobedience. (Hebrews 4:3-6,9-11, New American Bible)

Thus, this clearly shows that the command to keep the seventh day Sabbath is in the New Testament. The New Testament also shows that only those who will not observe it because of their disobedience argue otherwise. Early Christians realized that the Sabbath was in place for God's people.

Even Origen of Alexandria understood some of this as he wrote:

> But what is the feast of the Sabbath except that which the apostle speaks, "There remaineth therefore a Sabbatism," that is, the observance of the Sabbath, by the people of God...let us see how the Sabbath ought to be observed by a Christian. On the Sabbath-day all worldly labors ought to be abstained from...give yourselves up to spiritual exercises, repairing to church, attending to sacred reading and instruction... this is the observance of the Christian Sabbath (Translated from Origen's Opera 2, Paris, 1733, Andrews J.N. in History of the Sabbath, 3rd edition, 1887, pp. 324-325).

One reason that many today do not understand this is that certain translators have intentionally mistranslated the Greek term *sabbatismos* (ςαββατισμός) which is specifically found in Hebrews 4:9 (Green JP. The Interlinear Bible, 2nd edition. Hendrickson Publishers, 1986, p. 930).

The Protestant KJV and NKJV mistranslate it, as does the CHANGED version of the Rheims New Testament, also known as the Challoner version (changed in the 18th century). All three of them mistranslate the word as 'rest.'

Yet, there is a different Greek term (*katapausin*), translated as 'rest' in the New Testament. *Sabbatismos* clearly refers to a 'sabbath-rest' and honest scholars will all admit that. Because of the mistranslations, most today do not realize that the seventh-day Sabbath was specifically enjoined for Christians in the New Testament.

If you are Roman Catholic, consider the following:

> **Codex Amiatinus** The most celebrated manuscript of the Latin vulgate Bible, remarkable as the best witness to the true text of St. Jerome... (Fenlon, John Francis. "Codex Amiatinus." The Catholic Encyclopedia. Vol. 4. New York: Robert Appleton Company, 1908)

Here is the Latin from the *Codex Amiatinus:*

9 itaque relinquitur sabbatismus populo Dei (Hebrews 4:9, *Codex Amiatinus*)

It should be clear, even to non-Latin readers, that Hebrews 4:9 is definitely talking about the Sabbath. Decades ago, a Protestant told this author that the reason he did not keep the seventh-day Sabbath was because it was not taught for Christians in the New Testament. So, he was handed an RSV Bible and told to read Hebrews 4. After doing so, he said because his grandmother was a "good Christian" in his view, and because she did not keep it, he felt that he should not. He failed to truly rely on the Bible, but instead relied on false tradition (cf. Mark 7:6-8). Sadly most who profess Christianity do not keep the seventh-day Sabbath and rely mainly on improper traditions, whether they realize it or not.

Notice something from the Jehovah's Witness's translation of scripture:

> 9 So there remains a sabbath-rest for the people of God. (Hebrews 4:9, NWT, 2013)

So, the Jehovah's Witnesses should know the truth about this commandment as well—but they also do not keep the Sabbath.

For those interested in another source, here is a translation of Hebrews 4:9 from the, *Eastern Peschitta,* which is an Aramaic text (Roth AG, Daniel BB. Aramaic English New Testament, 5th edition. Netazari Press, 2012):

> 9. For there remains a Shabat for the people of Elohim.

Here is a claimed translation from a 'Hebrew' New Testament (which some call the Brit HaHadashah):

> 9 There remaineth therefore a sabbath rest for the people of God.

Whether we look at translations from the Greek, the early Latin Vulgate, Aramaic, or Hebrew, it should be clear that the Bible does enjoin Sabbath-keeping for Christians.

Although the Sabbath is a time of refreshing rest, many ignore that and consider it a burden. Notice the following prophecy that seems to apply to those who do not keep the Sabbath:

> 11 For with stammering lips and another tongue He will speak to this people, 12 To whom He said, "This is the rest with which You may cause the weary to rest," And, "This is the refreshing"; Yet they would not hear. (Isaiah 28:11-12)

Will you hear?

The seventh-day Sabbath remains for the true people of God.

Keeping the Sabbath

Keeping the Sabbath shows and builds faith. One trusts that God will provide if one is honoring God and truly keeping His commandments.

The Sabbath is kept from sunset on the day commonly called Friday through sunset on the day commonly called Saturday.

It is kept by doing the work we need to for six days (Exodus 20:9; cf. 2 Thessalonians 3:1-12) and then resting on the seventh (Exodus 20:10).

Christians should pray, meditate, and study the word of God on the Sabbath. Part of how we rest on the Sabbath is not going to our jobs or secular classes then nor doing carnal work nor classwork then.

Christians are to meet with, and encourage, others (Hebrew 10:24-25). The Sabbath is to be a holy convocation (Leviticus 23:2), which means that we attend church services if possible (we do not attend if we are ill and may infect others).

Because of distance, if one cannot attend with others, church services can be done alone with watching appropriate sermon and sermonette videos, etc. (the weekly *Letter to the Brethren* of the Continuing Church of God has a suggested Sabbath service format for scattered individuals who have internet access— while it is emailed out, it can also be found at www.ccog.org).

While one should not spend the entire Sabbath discussing carnal matters, and there are various matters that should not be discussed until after the Sabbath is over, one does not need to limit all conversations to only spiritual matters.

But also, notice the following:

> 13 "If you turn away your foot from the Sabbath,
> From doing your pleasure on My holy day,
> And call the Sabbath a delight,
> The holy day of the Lord honorable,
> And shall honor Him, not doing your own ways,
> Nor finding your own pleasure,
> Nor speaking your own words,
> 14 Then you shall delight yourself in the Lord;
> And I will cause you to ride on the high hills of the earth,
> And feed you with the heritage of Jacob your father.
> The mouth of the Lord has spoken." (Isaiah 58:13-14)

The Sabbath is to be called a delight. Yet, many who profess Christ call it an unnecessary burden.

Christians are spiritually Israelites (cf. Romans 2:28-29; Revelation 3:7-9) and heirs to the promises (Galatians 3:9). So, notice that the promises to Israel (Jacob) can be ours if we properly keep God's Sabbath, His Holy Day.

We are not to pursue carnal pursuits on the Sabbath (cf. Isaiah 58:13). Hence, we do not engage in sports, watch worldly entertainment, go shopping (though there could be an emergency), engage in physical exercise, etc. on the Sabbath. However, that does not mean one cannot take a walk or appreciate aspects of God's creation on the Sabbath.

Some have been confused about cooking. Cooking can be done on the Sabbath, as can bathing/showering. The commands against kindling a fire in the Old Testament (Exodus 35:3) had to do with industrial fires and not cooking:

> **Ye shall kindle no fire throughout your habitations upon the sabbath day.** The Sabbath was not a fast day. The Israelites cooked their victuals on that day, for which, of course, a fire would be necessary; and this view of the institution is supported by the conduct of our Lord (Luke 14:1) ... As the kindling of a fire, therefore, could only be for secular purposes (Jamieson, Fausset, and Brown Commentary).

So, cooking and food preparation can be appropriate (cf. Exodus 12:6). But one should not work oneself hard to cook on the Sabbath. Keep the Sabbath day holy.

Jesus also said that traveling can affect food acquisition on the Sabbath (Mark 2:23-26), and we will often eat out then if we are out-of-town.

Jesus taught that we are to do good on the Sabbath (Matthew 12:12).

While it is needful to take care of children and livestock (Luke 13:15) on the Sabbath, just because it may be the "busy season" at work does not mean that a Christian should violate the Sabbath to do carnal work (Exodus 34:21).

While Jesus said the work of God can be done on the Sabbath (cf. Matthew 12:5), this does not mean normal physical work. Though certain emergency situations can be handled (Luke 14:4). Yet, one should prepare for the Sabbath and reduce the possibility of such 'emergencies.'

Family Matters and Pleasures

As far as children go, this author and his wife have raised three, one of whom still lives with us. The other two, who have moved out of the house, still keep the Sabbath.

We would teach them, throughout the week, but more about the Bible on the Sabbath. We tried to instruct them as God commands (Deuteronomy 6:6-7).

We also tried to not make the Sabbath an unnecessarily difficult burden for them. But that also does not mean that we were particularly liberal with our rules either.

Unlike some parents, we did not take them to restaurants on the Sabbath (unless we were traveling), did not allow them (or ourselves) to watch television for entertainment, nor did we allow them to play secular video games.

We did, however, allow them to play Bible-based video games, which tended to be more like quizzes.

That is probably one of the reasons that our oldest son ended up developing various games/quizzes that are linked to the cogwriter.com website.

We did sometimes have livestock and we would tend to share the tasks of feeding and/or milking on the Sabbath (we never had more than one or two goats to milk). We would also tend to share other tasks that might have been needful on the Sabbath, such as meal preparation. But not massively time-consuming/complicated meal preparation, but also not intentionally plain meals either.

Of course, as we did not shop on the Sabbath, go to school on the Sabbath, nor go to work on the Sabbath, neither did our children.

It should also be noted that we all have some (or a lot of) formal education, and never did we do school-work or attend classes on the Sabbath. It is not that it was always easy, but the point is to state that it can be done--although in cultures with required or nearly required attendance on the Sabbath, this can be a much more difficult challenge, but there are also others who report that they successfully were able to handle this.

We also did allow our children, when young, to sometimes play outside with friends. We also would sometimes take our children to a park and sometimes take them to the beach. We tried to keep the Sabbath as a pleasant and holy day. Unlike some children brought up in various Church of God groups, our children did NOT dread the coming of the Sabbath nor do we (author and his wife) recall our children ever complaining about keeping the Sabbath.

As far as adults go, since this subject has come up before, based upon the fact that the weekly Sabbath is not a regular time to fast as well as various scriptures (e.g. 1 Corinthians 7:3-4), marital relations are not forbidden on the Sabbath.

All people should attend services on the Sabbath, with others when possible:

> 24 And let us consider one another in order to stir up love and good works, 25 not forsaking the assembling of ourselves together, as is the manner of some, but exhorting one another, and so much the more as you see the Day approaching. (Hebrews 10:24-25)

Christians are not to just focus on themselves, but should exhort other Christians as we get closer to the return of Jesus and the establishment of the millennial kingdom of God.

The Sabbath helps picture the millennial reign. Because of statements, various scriptures, Jews (Psalm 90:4; Psalm 92) and early Christians (2 Peter 3:8; Hebrews 4:6-8; Revelation 20:4-6) believed that the Sabbath helped picture the millennium. Essentially, they taught that the six days of physical creation represented six one-thousand year days, followed by the Sabbath, representing the millennial rest. Jewish tradition also seemingly attributes statements by Elijah confirming this (Babylonian Talmud: Sanhedrin 97a).

Even Greco-Roman-Protestant saint Irenaeus realized this as he wrote:

> These are [to take place] in the times of the kingdom, that is, upon the seventh day, which has been sanctified, in which God rested from all the works which He created, which is the true Sabbath of the righteous, which they shall not be engaged in any earthly occupation; but shall have a table at hand prepared for them by God, supplying them with all sorts of dishes (Against Heresies. Book V, Chapter 33, Verse 2)

So did the 4th century Greco-Roman saint and bishop Methodius:

> For I also, taking my journey, and going forth from the Egypt of this life, came first to the resurrection, which is the true Feast of the Tabernacles, and there having set up my tabernacle, adorned with the fruits of virtue, on the first day of the resurrection, which is the day of judgment, celebrate with Christ the millennium of rest, which is called the seventh day, even the true Sabbath. (Methodius. Banquet of the Ten Virgins, Discourse 9, chapter 5)

Jerome observed that 5th century Sabbath-keeping Christians also believed that the seven-day Feast of

Tabernacles also pictured the millennium (Jerome, Commentariorum in Zachariam Lib. III. Patrologia Latina 25, 1529; 1536). One interesting aspect of this is that the Bible teaches that the Book of Deuteronomy is to be read every seven years during the Feast of Tabernacles (Deuteronomy 31:10-13), and that includes reading the version of the Ten Commandments listed in its 5th chapter.

The Bible teaches that the millennial reign will be a fantastic time and that the law will be taught then (Isaiah 2:2-4; Micah 4:1-4) with reminders given by God's teachers to observe it (Isaiah 30:20-21).

The Sabbath is a weekly reminder that God's millennial kingdom will come.

In this current age, the Sabbath is to be a blessing:

> 1 Thus says the Lord: "Keep justice, and do righteousness, For My salvation is about to come, And My righteousness to be revealed. 2 Blessed is the man who does this, And the son of man who lays hold on it; Who keeps from defiling the Sabbath, And keeps his hand from doing any evil." (Isaiah 56:1-2)

The Bible teaches that ALL of God's "commandments are righteousness" (Psalm 119:172), and that obviously includes the Sabbath as Isaiah 56:1-2 points out.

The righteous keep the Sabbath.

Fourth Commandment Before Sinai, from Jesus, and After Jesus' Death

The Bible shows the fourth commandment was in place before Mt. Sinai:

> "And on the seventh day God ended His work which He had done, and He rested on the seventh day from all His work which He had done. Then God blessed the seventh day and sanctified it, because in it He rested from all His work which God had created and made" (Genesis 2:2-3). "Is there not a time of hard service for man on the earth" (Job 7:1). "the triumphing of the wicked is short...Because he knows no quietness in his heart" (Job 20:5,20). "Tomorrow is a Sabbath rest, a holy Sabbath to the LORD ... How long do you refuse to keep My commandments and My laws? See! For the Lord has given you the Sabbath ... So the people rested on the seventh day" (Exodus 16:23, 28-30). "The Sabbath was made for man" (Mark 2:27).

Jesus taught and expanded the fourth commandment:

> "What man is there among you who has one sheep, and it falls into a pit on the Sabbath, will not lay hold of it and lift it out? Of how much more value then is a man than a sheep? Therefore, it is lawful to do good on the Sabbath" (Matthew 12:11-12). "And pray that your flight may not be in winter or on the Sabbath" (Matthew 24:20); there would be no reason to pray this if the Sabbath was not going to be in existence. "And He said to them, 'The Sabbath was made for man, and not man for the Sabbath. Therefore the Son of Man is also Lord of the Sabbath'" (Mark 2:27); this verse tells all who will see which day is the Lord's Day. "And when the Sabbath had come, He began to teach in the synagogue" (Mark 6:2). "And as His custom was, He went into the synagogue on the Sabbath day, and stood up to read" (Luke 4:16). "Then He went down to Capernaum, a city of Galilee, and was teaching them on the Sabbaths" (Luke 4:31). "The Son of Man is also Lord of the Sabbath...Is it lawful on the Sabbath to do good or to do evil, to save life or to destroy?" (Luke 6:5,9). "But the ruler of the synagogue answered with indignation, because Jesus had healed on the Sabbath...The Lord then answered him and said, 'Hypocrite...So ought not this woman...be loosed from this bond on the Sabbath?'" (Luke 13:14-16). "'Is it lawful to heal on the Sabbath?'...And they could not answer Him regarding these things" (Luke 14:3,6). "are you angry with Me because I made a man completely well on the Sabbath?" (John 7:23).

Jesus did not 'do away with the Sabbath.' Jesus eliminated extra 'traditions' that the Pharisees added to the Sabbath commandment. He emphasized that the Sabbath was for doing good.

Jesus never taught that the Sabbath was supposed to

be on Sunday.

After Jesus was resurrected, the New Testament taught the fourth commandment:

> "Then Paul, as his custom was, went in to them and for three Sabbaths reasoned with them from the Scriptures...And he reasoned in the synagogue every Sabbath, and persuaded both Jews and Greeks" (Acts 17:2;18:4 see also 13:14,27,42,44). "let him labor, working with his hands what is good, that he may have something to give to him who has need" (Ephesians 4:28) and "For even when we were with you, we commanded you this: 'If anyone will not work, neither shall he eat'" (2 Thessalonians 3:10); (recall that the requirement to work is also part of the Sabbath command, thus even that portion of the commandment is repeated in the New Testament.) "And to whom did He swear they would not enter His rest, but to those who did not obey?" (Hebrews 3:18). "For He has spoken in a certain place of the seventh day in this way: 'And God rested on the seventh day from all His works'" (Hebrews 4:4). "There remains therefore a rest (literally sabbatismos, 'Sabbath rest') for the people of God. For he who has entered His rest has himself also ceased from his works as God did from His" (Hebrews 4:9-10). That day was the Preparation and the Sabbath drew near...And they rested on the Sabbath in accordance with the commandment" (Luke 23:54,56). "But when they departed from Perga, they came to Antioch in Pisidia, and went into the synagogue on the Sabbath day and sat down" (Acts 13:14), they seemed to be following this admonition from John, "He who says he abides in Him ought also to walk just as He walked" (I John 2:6), since Jesus always went to the synagogues on the Sabbath (Luke 4:16), Christians are to keep the Sabbath.

No one in the New Testament is shown teaching that Sunday was the replacement for Saturday.

The late Roman Catholic Cardinal James Gibbons wrote:

> You may read the Bible from Genesis to Revelation, and you will not find a single line authorizing the sanctification of Sunday. The Scriptures enforce the religious observance of Saturday, a day which we never sanctify. (Gibbons J., Cardinal. The faith of our fathers: being a plain exposition and vindication of the church founded by Our Lord Jesus Chris, 83rd reprint edition. P.J. Kenedy, 1917, pp. 72-73)

The seventh-day Sabbath, and not Sunday, is the day of rest in the Bible, and even Catholic leaders know this.

Those willing to "live by ... every word that proceeds from the mouth of God" (Matthew 4:4) keep the seventh-day Sabbath.

More on the Ten Commandments can be found in our free online book, available at www.ccog.org, titled: 'The Ten Commandments: The Decalogue, Christianity, and the Beast.'

FREE *Continuing Church of God* Books and Booklets

at www.ccog.org/books

Christians: AMBASSADORS

Continuing History of the Church of God

Dating: A Key to Success in Marriage

Faith for Those God has Called and Chosen

STUDY THE BIBLE COURSE

Lesson 16a: You Must Be Born Again

Published 2019 by the *Continuing* Church of God

> Preface: This course is highly based upon the personal correspondence course developed in 1954 that began under the direction of the late C. Paul Meredith in the old Radio Church of God. Various portions have been updated for the 21st century (though much of the original writing has been retained). It also has more scriptural references, as well as information and questions not in the original course. Unless otherwise noted, scriptural references are to the NKJV, copyright Thomas Nelson Publishing, used by permission. The KJV, sometimes referred to as the Authorized Version is also often used. Additionally, Catholic-approved translations such as the New Jerusalem Bible (NJB) are sometimes used as are other translations.

SOME of the teachings in the Bible are a little hard to understand.

James tells us to count it all joy when trials, ordeals, and reverses beset us (James 1:2).

TROUBLES a JOY? That's pretty hard to accept, isn't it? And, for the average person, a lot harder to put into practice.

Few find any pleasure, let alone JOY, in the obstacles and troubles they encounter. Yet this Biblical teaching says we ought so to count them. There is a REASON, although FEW understand it.

In Psalm 34:19 you'll read that the righteous are going to have to bear MANY afflictions. But, it promises, the Eternal will deliver us out of them all – IF we believe and trust Him!

Again, it is through MUCH TRIBULATION that we must enter the Kingdom of God (Acts 14:22, KJV). WHY? There's a reason!

Now consider another Biblical teaching hard for some to understand.

In the fifth chapter of Ephesians, verses 22-23, you find a husband-wife relationship pictured as corresponding to Christ and the Church. Scriptural teaching assures us that, at His coming, Christ is going to MARRY the Church (2 Corinthians 11:1–2; Revelation 19:7). Also the Scriptures teach that the Church will, at His coming, be BORN of God, by a resurrection of all who have died, and the instantaneous conversion from mortal to immortal of those then living (1 Corinthians 15:50-53).

So one person reasons: Could a full-grown MAN marry an infant girl baby, just born? If those in the Church are to be just then BORN of God, how can they marry Christ before they grow up?

This, too, seems difficult for some to comprehend. Yet the answer to James' teaching – the UNDERSTANDING of what James really means, is also the answer to this seeming inconsistency.

There is a third seeming inconsistency, hard for some to understand. Contrary to the thinking of many, a Christian may – and too often does – actually commit sin AFTER conversion. Christians SHOULD NOT, of course. But too often they do, and still remain Christian. The true explanation of James' teaching, first mentioned above, is also the explanation of this experience.

So LET'S UNDERSTAND!

WHY were we born, in the first place? What is the real PURPOSE of human life? To give love in a unique way and to make eternity better.

To expand those who can do so, God Almighty

the Creator is reproducing Himself! As truly as we mortal humans have been given power to reproduce ourselves – to bring forth progeny in our own image, born with our very nature even so the Great God is bringing forth sons in HIS image, born with His very divine nature!

The very PURPOSE of our existence is that we, being begotten as God's children will develop godly character in this age, so that we can become BORN of Him and then be able to best give and increase love and make eternity better.

And human reproduction is the very type of spiritual reproduction. What God created at the time described in the first chapter of Genesis was a PHYSICAL creation. You'll find nothing spiritual there. In physical man, made of the dust of the ground, God created the MATERIAL WITH WHICH He may mold, shape, form, and create the SPIRITUAL being. He pictures us as the clay, Himself as the Potter – forming us into the spiritual image of HIS designing.

Now human reproduction, in a sense, pictures spiritual reproduction. Each human, since Adam and Eve, started from a tiny egg, called an ovum, the size of a pinpoint. It was produced in the body of the mother. The egg is INCOMPLETE, of itself. It has a life of only about 12-24 hours, according to some authorities. Unless fertilized by the life-giving sperm cell from the human father within that limited lifetime, it dies.

Each human, spiritually speaking, is like an egg. The average human lifetime is said to be 70 or 80 years (Psalm 90:10). Adam was created INCOMPLETE, and each of us was BORN INCOMPLETE – that is, we were made to NEED the Holy Spirit of God. And unless, within our limited life-span we are begotten of God – by His Spirit which is HIS IMMORTAL DIVINE LIFE entering to impart eternal life to us, we shall die and that would be the end. Except that God has appointed a resurrection of all who have lived, and, for those who reject His gift of eternal life, the final second death in the lake of fire.

But, in the case of the human ovum, once fertilized as a begotten human, the egg – now called an embryo – is kept within the body of the mother and is nourished and fed material food through her and protected by her. And there it must grow – being fed physically through the mother – large enough to be born. After a number of weeks, the embryo is called a fetus, and at birth it is a human baby.

In like manner, the Bible indicates that the truly faithful CHURCH, which began in Jerusalem, is the "mother of us all" (Galatians 4:24-31). That is, the mother of Christians (Revelation 12:17) – those begotten of God. It is the function of the Church to protect and feed (Matthew 28:19-20; Ephesians 4:11-16), spiritually, on the spiritual food of GOD'S WORD, those begotten children of God, so that we may GROW SPIRITUALLY (1 Peter 2:1-2; 2 Peter 3:18), in the divine character, ready to be born.

Surely this is a wonderful comparison. Yet types and ante-types are not always alike in every detail.

When a physical baby is born, it is not ready for marriage. When the spiritual children of God are BORN, they will be fully mature for the spiritual marriage. How can this be? This is what one thinking person could not see.

The unborn human fetus is only growing PHYSICALLY. At birth, the human baby knows nothing. The baby is helpless. The baby must be taught. The baby must learn. The baby is born merely with a mind CAPABLE of learning, knowing, thinking. The baby is not yet of mature size physically or mentally. Many do marry who are still entirely immature spiritually and/or emotionally. But we do assume that one has reached reasonable maturity physically and mentally before marriage. In the human, this development takes place in the human state AFTER the human birth.

Therefore, the human baby is not ready for marriage at birth.

But the spirit-born are different!

Just as the fertilized ovum – the embryo which becomes the fetus – must grow PHYSICALLY from material food, so the spirit-begotten child of God must grow SPIRITUALLY before he can be born. BUT THERE IS A DIFFERENCE!

The fetus does not attain to complete physical

MATURITY before birth, and has no mental maturity. But, in the spiritual rebirth, one must attain reasonable spiritual maturity BEFORE he is spirit-born.

Now what IS spiritual growth? Just as the physical embryo-fetus must GROW physically large enough to be BORN, so the Spirit-begotten Christian must grow SPIRITUALLY or the fetus will never be BORN of God. But spiritual growth is CHARACTER-DEVELOPMENT.

The Spirit-begotten starts out with a MIND from the beginning. God IS perfect character – divine, spiritual character. God is also LOVE. And perfect spiritual character is THE WAY of LOVE! Such a character is the attainment of the ability, in a separate independent entity of free moral agency, to be able to discern right from wrong – the true values from the false truth from error – the right way from the wrong; and then to make the right CHOICE or DECISION, even against self-desire, impulse or temptation; plus the WILL and self-discipline to resist the wrong and to DO the right.

No human, with human nature, has the power – of oneself – to do this. But God has made AVAILABLE the spiritual power and help humans lack. People must desire to KNOW – must hunger and thirst for truth; humans must make their own individual decision, exercise will, even against the pulls of human nature. But without the help of God – without spiritual POWER from God – all are utterly unable.

That is why truly converted Christians sometimes actually DO SIN. They are like the apostle Paul, as he describes himself in Romans 7. With his mind he WANTED to go the way of God's law, yet he found himself unable. Another law – human nature warred within him against the good resolutions of his mind. But the sequel to Romans 7 is Romans 8 – the Holy Spirit chapter. WHO, Paul cried out, could save him from this body of death he struggled against in vain? The answer is, GOD, through His Holy Spirit.

Sometimes the sin is so within one that it seems to defy human will. Notice some of what the Apostle Paul wrote:

> 15 For what I am doing, I do not understand. For what I will to do, that I do not practice; but what I hate, that I do. 16 If, then, I do what I will not to do, I agree with the law that it is good. 17 But now, it is no longer I who do it, but sin that dwells in me. 18 For I know that in me (that is, in my flesh) nothing good dwells; for to will is present with me, but how to perform what is good I do not find. 19 For the good that I will to do, I do not do; but the evil I will not to do, that I practice. 20 Now if I do what I will not to do, it is no longer I who do it, but sin that dwells in me.
>
> 21 I find then a law, that evil is present with me, the one who wills to do good. 22 For I delight in the law of God according to the inward man. 23 But I see another law in my members, warring against the law of my mind, and bringing me into captivity to the law of sin which is in my members. 24 O wretched man that I am! Who will deliver me from this body of death? 25 I thank God — through Jesus Christ our Lord! (Romans 7:15-25)

Jesus also said, "with men it is impossible, but with God all things are possible" (Matthew 19:26).

We all have lost the struggle with sin at times, but through Christ we can overcome.

Jesus was tempted as we are and understands:

> 14 Seeing then that we have a great High Priest who has passed through the heavens, Jesus the Son of God, let us hold fast our confession. 15 For we do not have a High Priest who cannot sympathize with our weaknesses, but was in all points tempted as we are, yet without sin. 16 Let us therefore come boldly to the throne of grace, that we may obtain mercy and find grace to help in time of need. (Hebrews 4:14-16)

No matter how much you feel you messed up, you still can boldly go to the throne of grace to obtain mercy.

> 13 I can do all things through Christ who strengthens me. (Philippians 4:13)

A true Christian doesn't want to sin – should not. But sometimes Christians find themselves caught in the vise of habit, or overwhelmed by temptation or by circumstances from which they seem unable to be free of. Surely, had such a one been CONTINUALLY praying, keeping CLOSE TO GOD, and detached from the world or its lures or the temptations of the flesh, then that Christian probably would have had sufficient divine help to have prevented the sinning (cf. Proverbs 3:5-6; 1 Corinthians 10:13; Philippians 4:13). But ONLY JESUS CHRIST ever did keep permanently close to God!

God looks on the heart. In such a case, the Christian does not sin maliciously, with malice aforethought. The person is merely caught in the vortex of a temptation which sucks the believer helplessly down into the sin. Then the Christian is terribly sorry. The Christian is disgusted with the wrong action and repents. The Christian goes to work to overcome. The Christian may not succeed, due to human weakness, at once. But the Christian remains determined and, finally, does, with God's help, overcome completely. Many a true Christian has had such a struggle over a particular human weakness and temptation, and after even several setbacks, finally, through God's power, won the victory and fought the way to be free.

God looks on the heart. God FORGIVES in such cases. The living Christ, our High Priest, has compassion, is filled with mercy – as long as the attitude is right, the DESIRE of the inner Christian is to conquer the flesh and overcome the temptation and be FREE from it entirely. In the end, it is GOD who gives the victory. But, in such a struggle, the Christian DEVELOPS CHARACTER.

Now character, is something God does not create automatically. It is DEVELOPED, against the opposing pulls of human nature, with the decisions and wills and struggles of the individual, and through EXPERIENCE.

Perfect, holy and righteous character is the ability in such separate entity to come to discern the true and right way from the false, to make voluntarily a full and unconditional surrender to God and His perfect way - to yield to be conquered by God - to determine even against temptation or self-desire, to live and to do the right. And even then such holy character is the gift of God. It comes by yielding to God to instill His law (God's right way of life) within the entity who so decides and wills.

The development of that CHARACTER is related to the very PURPOSE of our being alive. Also the development of that character, unlike the purely physical growth of the unborn baby, actually is growth toward SPIRITUAL MATURITY, right now in the BEGETTAL stage prior to spirit BIRTH – in this present mortal human life.

Now, once BEGOTTEN of God do we then stop growing spiritually? Consider, once a human grows up to human maturity, does the person then STOP growing? Physically, yes – but mentally, morally, spiritually, emotionally the person SHOULD continue to grow and develop as long as he/she lives. Perhaps many humans don't. But we all SHOULD. Adults who have reached this physical maturity should still learn new things continually.

If you are meeting problems and trials, don't be discouraged. Take them to CHRIST for wisdom and power and help. Have FAITH. And count it all JOY! And NEVER quit or give up! Have perseverance!

When you were begotten by your parents, you were unborn, but your mother was still your mother. She nourished you while you were developing in the womb, until you reached sufficient maturity to be born (presuming no health complications).

Consider that the "mother of us all," the Church, is to protect and FEED those in it, until they reach spiritual MATURITY. In I Corinthians 12, you'll read how God gives spiritual gifts for various administrations, or functions of service. In Ephesians 4:11-14, Christ has given special spiritual abilities or talents to certain ones in a chain of authority under Him in the Church – and notice for what PURPOSE:

> 11 And He Himself gave some to be apostles, some prophets, some evangelists, and some pastors and teachers, 12 for the equipping of the saints for the work of ministry, for the edifying of the body of Christ, 13 till we all come to the unity of the faith and of the knowledge of the Son of God, to a perfect man, to the measure of the stature of the fullness of Christ; (Ephesians 4:11-13, RSV).

In other words, TC FULL SPIRITUAL MATURITY!

Now WHY should we count the troubles and problems and temptations that beset us as all JOY?

Simply because we CANNOT hurdle these obstacles successfully in our own power. They drive us to seek help from God. To go to God for the wisdom to know WHAT to do, and the power to be able to do it, requires FAITH. This is a LIVING faith. It is ALIVE. It is active.

When we meet such trials, we often do not know what to do. We lack the WISDOM to make the right decision. So open your Bible to the first chapter of James. Notice verses 5-6.

If you lack wisdom, in such trials, GO TO GOD for it! But ask IN FAITH -- no wavering – no doubting. Be SURE God will not fail, but will give you this wisdom. Depend upon Him for it. If you waver, you are like a wave in the ocean – tossed back and forth – going nowhere! So, instead of wavering, BE STEADFAST. And if you don't get the answer immediately from God, have PATIENCE. Don't give up. Trust Him.

Now notice verses 2-3: "Count it all JOY, my brethren, when you meet various trials, for you know that the testing of your faith produces steadfastness" (James 1:2-3, RSV). These trials force you to your knees. You must have FAITH to meet them. They TEST your faith. They DEVELOP spiritual CHARACTER!

In the King James version, it says the trying of your faith produces patience. It produces that kind of patience that is steadfastness. THAT IS CHARACTER! Sure, it may be unpleasant for a while. But, Paul assures us that if we suffer with Christ, we shall REIGN with Him – and the GLORY TO BE revealed in us is so incomparably greater than anything we now are, that this promised future for eternity is something to REJOICE over!

Yes, count it all JOY! Even if unpleasant. It is maturing you, now, for the marriage to Christ. The true members of the CHURCH of God shall be BORN the KINGDOM OF GOD! The Kingdom of God will not be composed of spiritual know-nothings and infants.

When we are born again – born of God – resurrected in spirit bodies, those bodies will not be small, like a human physical infant which must GROW to full physical size. We shall LOOK as we do now, so far as form and shape and features are concerned. But the resurrected body will be a DIFFERENT body – composed of SPIRIT instead of flesh and blood (1 Corinthians 15:35-44).

The original twelve apostles were Christ's WITNESSES. That is, they were actual eyewitnesses that Jesus rose from the dead – that the living resurrected Christ was the SAME Jesus who had been crucified. They were with Him forty days after His resurrection. But nobody will be foolish enough to suggest that when Christ was BORN very Son of God by the resurrection (Romans 1:4) that He was resurrected in a tiny infant's body composed of spirit. He was resurrected FULL GROWN, as He had been when crucified. How did the apostles KNOW He was the SAME Jesus? Because they knew what Jesus had looked like – and in His born-again resurrected body HE LOOKED THE SAME, except He now was composed of SPIRIT instead of matter!

The resurrected Christ was PERFECT – He was very God! But He did not grow up into perfection AFTER He was resurrected. It was during His human lifetime, setting us the example, that He WAS MADE PERFECT as you read in Hebrews 2:10 and 5:8-9.

Thus it is plain that we must develop spiritual character, growing to spiritual adulthood, DURING THIS LIFE – not after our resurrection in GLORY! THIS IS the SPIRITUAL growth, of which the PHYSICAL growth of the unborn child, from tiny embryo to a size and weight of some six to eight pounds at birth, is a type. The physical growth of the unborn human is a growth of physical size and weight. The SPIRITUAL growth of the begotten, but yet unborn SPIRITUAL child of God is a growth in spiritual CHARACTER, not of physical volume, size or weight. The human baby merely grows large enough to be born prior to birth – NOT TO PHYSICAL OR MENTAL MATURITY. But the child DOES GROW. And this physical growth is the TYPE of the spiritual growth by feeding on the Word of God, and prayer, and Christian fellowship, and participation in the Work of God in the life of the begotten child of God.

The DIFFERENCE IS merely the difference between matter and spirit. One is a material growth. Material growth is measured by volume, size, weight. The other is spiritual growth, measured by character development.

Jesus was BORN a very Son of God by His resurrection (Romans 1:4). He was born fully MATURE. He was born in a spirit body, which was manifested to His apostles in the same apparent size and shape as when He died. When He appears on earth the second time, in His spirit glorified body, we shall be resurrected, or instantaneously changed, into a body that will be LIKE HIM (1 John 3:1-2).

At that instant, our present mortal physical VILE bodies will be CHANGED like unto His glorified body. BUT upon conversion in this life, our vile carnal CHARACTERS are not suddenly and totally changed.

Our CHARACTER must be changed, and developed to spiritual adulthood NOW, during THIS life. Otherwise we simply shall not be then born of God!

But all who are then born of God will be born as spiritual beings! Yes, ready for the marriage to Christ! If we NOW overcome, we shall reign with Christ (Revelation 3:21; 2:26-27). We shall be married to Him! We shall be BORN SPIRITUALLY MATURE. This development to spiritual maturity is precisely what IS spiritual GROWTH sufficient to be born.

The Bible reveals that you were born for a tremendous purpose. But few really grasp the magnitude of the awesome future God offers mankind.

Believe it or not, you were born to rule in love and make eternity better!

Just as surely as a crown prince born into a royal family is to be a king, you are destined, when 'born again' into the universe-ruling Family of God, to reign as an even greater and eternal king.

Incredible as it may sound, your Bible reveals that you were born to ultimately help rule the universe (cf. Hebrews 2:6-8).

WHAT it means to be 'Born Again'!

Last century (the practice is not nearly as common now), on some American street corners and especially in evangelistic campaigns, you might hear ministers ask, "Brother, have you been 'born again'? Just believe, and give the preacher your hand and the Lord your heart, and you'll be a 'born again' child of God." But is that all there is to being 'born again'? True, YOUR BIBLE DOES TEACH THAT YOU MUST BE 'BORN AGAIN.' But it also teaches that there is much more you must do before this happy event can happen to you than 'just believe, and give the preacher your hand.'

Neither do these ministers tell you WHY YOU need to be 'born again'! LET'S UNDERSTAND this whole matter of 'rebirth'!

WHY You Must Be Born Again

Humans were born without the vital essence that will enable them to live forever. Humans are mortal. Humans are breathing, blood-circulating, temporarily existing material beings. Humans are subject to death. And this includes you!

Your time is fast running out, second by second. There is NO ETERNAL LIFE IN YOU as a result of your first birth. Your parents did not have immortality to give to you. You are exactly like any animal at death (Ecclesiastes 3:19).

You were born a mortal flesh-and-blood being composed of matter, with the probability of living some seventy or eighty years.

WHAT YOU NEED IS TO BE BORN AGAIN, this time as an immortal being composed of spirit – with INHERENT eternal life so you can't die!

God Created Humans Mortal

God formed our first parents, not out of spirit, but 'of the dust of the ground.' To the man whose creation is described in Genesis 1:26 and 2:7, God said, "For dust you are" (Genesis 3:19) NOT immortal spirit – just DUST. Humankind is still MORTAL, not yet immortal!

Adam was a perfect PHYSICAL specimen, yes! Whatever God creates is perfect, not imperfect. But what God created, in Adam, was a FLESHLY man – a MORTAL man of flesh and blood! He was the perfect 'clay model' with which, by now adding a spiritual ingredient and reshaping his character, the Master Potter purposes to CREATE a reproduction of His glorious self!

Adam, in other words, was not complete! One vital thing was lacking – and this one thing he was made to need – to hunger and to thirst for – the indwelling of God's HOLY SPIRIT!

WHY We Need the Holy Spirit

We inherited mortal life through Adam. But we can become HEIRS of ETERNAL LIFE – heirs of God and the Kingdom of God – by being SPIRITUALLY begotten by the HOLY SPIRIT, which is the eternal LIFE of God. "And this is the testimony: that God has given us eternal life, and this life is in His SON" – NOT in an 'immortal soul' we are SUPPOSED to possess. " He who has the Son HAS LIFE; he who does not have the Son of God DOES NOT HAVE LIFE. These things I have written to you," says John, "that you may know that you have eternal life" (1 John 5:11-13).

Eternal life with unending spiritual power is A GIFT OF GOD. It is an attribute of the Holy Spirit. "For the wages of sin is death, but the [free] gift of God is eternal life" (Romans 6:23). If we already had eternal life, it would NOT be a gift; it would be INHERITED from our physical parents.

Notice the RESULT of having the Holy Spirit: "Now if any man have not the Spirit of Christ [the Holy Spirit] he is none of his. And if Christ be IN YOU" – living the same life IN US now by the HOLY SPIRIT, as HE lived by the Holy Spirit while He was personally on earth – "the body is dead" – i.e., dying – "because of sin; but the SPIRIT IS LIFE because of righteousness. But if the Spirit of him" – the Father – "that raised up Jesus from the dead DWELL IN you, he that raised up Christ from the dead shall also QUICKEN" – make immortal – "your mortal bodies by his Spirit that dwelleth in you (Romans 8:9-11, KJV).

How plain. If the Holy Spirit dwells in us, we will ultimately receive ETERNAL LIFE as Jesus did!
BUT HAVING THE HOLY SPIRIT NOW DOES MORE than impart THE POWER TO COMMENCE ETERNAL LIFE in us. It imparts to us the CHARACTERISTICS of the Almighty, the all-powerful God the Father.

A Different Nature, Too

You also need a different NATURE SO YOU will not continue to live eternally in sin, suffering and misery. The human nature which causes you to sin and brings upon you the death penalty must be replaced by a new and different nature, the DIVINE NATURE of God which cannot sin (1 John 3:9).

God the Father has PERFECT CHARACTER, perfect control over Himself. That is what you need. But you weren't born with such powers. The only way to have God's character developed in you is to receive within your mind the Spirit of God – the divine nature of God. The only One who has both eternal life, and perfect character, is God. You NEED TO BE BORN OF GOD! But how?

How Is Rebirth Possible?

About two thousand years ago Nicodemus, a ruler of the Jews, was puzzled by this question like you probably are. Jesus had told him, "unless one is BORN AGAIN, he cannot see the kingdom of God." (John 3:3) Nicodemus understood the true meaning of the word 'born.' But he still couldn't understand how it could be possible to be born once AGAIN, to have another life. "HOW can a man be born when he is old? Can he enter a second time into his mother's womb and be [re-] born?" he asked Jesus (verse 4).

Nicodemus knew only of a physical birth from physical parents. Therefore Jesus said to Nicodemus, "That which is born of the flesh IS FLESH" (verse 6). Then He explained we must be born AGAIN – NOT again of the FLESH – NOT again by entering our mother's womb, as Nicodemus thought He meant – but be born of the Spirit – born of God! GOD must be our FATHER this time! As we were born of the flesh from fleshly human parents, so now we must be born of the Spirit of our heavenly Spiritual Father.

Here are TWO DIFFERENT KINDS OF BIRTH, ONE PHYSICAL, THE OTHER SPIRITUAL. When you were born of your FLESHLY parents you were COMPOSED OF FLESH. Your father and mother passed on to you a FLESHLY NATURE at birth. But, unlike that birth, the SECOND birth is not a physical, fleshly one, but a SPIRITUAL BIRTH!

Just as a human being is flesh because he was born of fleshly parents, Jesus declared that anyone born again of SPIRIT IS COMPOSED OF SPIRIT – he IS SPIRIT, no longer flesh! "that which is born of the Spirit is spirit" (verse 6) and NOT flesh. There will be no blood in his body. He will not have to breathe air to exist. That's the plain teaching of the Bible!

The new birth is NOT an emotional experience, but A LITERAL BIRTH. SO YOU would not mistake the true meaning of being born of the Spirit, Jesus explained that as "The wind blows where it wishes [where it wills], and you hear the sound of it, but cannot tell where it comes from and where it goes. So is everyone who is BORN of the Spirit." (verse 8)

Notice what Scripture says. WHEN YOU ARE 'BORN FROM ABOVE,' BORN OF THE HEAVENLY Father – GOD – YOU WILL BE INVISIBLE like the wind which human eyes can't see. The work of the wind is easily discernible, but the wind itself cannot be seen. Also, if you were already 'born again,' as the common teaching is, you would possess the FULL MEASURE of the NATURE of your heavenly Father – which, of course, you do NOT!

Jesus compared the physical birth to the Spiritual one. The former is a type of the latter. Human parents pass on a fleshly nature at birth to their children; so with our Heavenly Parent. God the Father impregnates or begets us with His Spirit at conversion when we desire, with all our heart, to turn from our old ways. He imparts to us His Spiritual nature which must grow through a lifetime until it finally COMPOSES our minds WHEN WE ARE BORN AGAIN. WE MUST GROW SPIRITUALLY, just as a human fetus must GROW physically before it can be born. If we don't grow, we become a 'miscarriage' and are NOT BORN again.

Born Again at the Resurrection

Obviously all human beings who claim to be BORN AGAIN, now at this time, are deceived – they are STILL flesh and blood. The new birth is something yet to occur AT THE RESURRECTION. Jesus said you must be born again, you must be composed of spirit in order to see or enter the Kingdom of God.

IN SPEAKING OF THE RESURRECTION in 1 Corinthians 15:50 the apostle Paul says, "Now this I say, brethren, that FLESH AND BLOOD CANNOT INHERIT THE KINGDOM of God; nor does corruption inherit incorruption."

Note that Paul preached to the Corinthians the very same doctrine that Jesus at first spoke to Nicodemus. You never can enter or inherit the Kingdom or Family of God unless you are born of God – composed of Spirit which DOES NOT DECAY.

Paul tells in the next verses WHEN the new birth of Christians will occur. "we shall all be changed" – no longer flesh and blood – "at THE LAST TRUMPET. For the trumpet will sound, and the dead will be raised". In verse 44, Paul says, "It is SOWN A NATURAL BODY" – your first birth was natural, physical, fleshly, but when you are BORN AGAIN "it is RAISED A SPIRITUAL BODY."

Notice it! Both Jesus and Paul speak of PHYSICAL AND SPIRITUAL BODIES. Jesus tells WHY YOU will be composed of spirit – in being born again you have the spirit body of your Parent, for LIKE PRODUCES LIKE. If you are BORN OF GOD, your Heavenly Father, you WILL BE SPIRIT – because God is Spirit – you will be composed of the same substance of which He is composed.

Paul tells us that THIS CHANGE from flesh to spirit TAKES PLACE AT THE RESURRECTION. Then you will be composed of spirit, PROVIDED YOU have been BEGOTTEN in this life and provided you have GROWN sufficiently in grace and knowledge and Godly character to be born of God.

Don't Be a Miscarriage!

Here is the terrible consequence of believing that people are already 'born again' because some preacher says so. Instead of GROWING as unborn babes NEED TO DO in order to be born, those who trust in a false new birth believe that there is no need of spiritual growth now, or obedience to the commandments, because they think they are already 'saved.' When the resurrection comes, such people will not be there! They will not have grown or developed into the stature of Jesus' character because of not having obeyed the commandments of God.

Do you want to follow the broad way and perish, like a MISCARRIAGE of a human fetus – a child that is conceived, but never born?

Or do you believe what Jesus said – that once 'converted,' or begotten by the Holy Spirit, you need to grow by every word of God which CLEANS YOU UP SPIRITUALLY, just as water cleans you physically (John 3:5; Ephesians 5:26), SO you can finally be born of God and inherit the kingdom of God?

'Born Again NOW' an Old and False Teaching

Because Jesus made the new birth essential to entering the kingdom of God, Satan has had some of his churches and his ministers preaching COUNTERFEIT 'NEW BIRTHS' to DECEIVE the people, and to make the true way appear false (2 Corinthians 11:14, 15).

Masquerading as ministers of righteousness, they have DELUDED MILLIONS –into accepting and appropriating the NAME of Jesus Christ, shedding a few tears and believing in a superstitious 'born again' experience.

Some make it a little more involved by working up an emotional ecstasy which is interpreted to mean 'regeneration,' 'sanctification,' 'baptism of the Holy Ghost,' and a 'new birth'!

Whatever the slight doctrinal differences, the devil has many CHURCHES DECEIVED into believing that Christians are already 'born again,' that everything is all set. There are 'NO WORKS,' as the saying goes. No need to obey God! There is no need, preach the false ministers, to obey God's commandments because you are already 'regenerated.'

This is SATAN'S CLEVER METHOD OF BEGUILING THE PEOPLE INTO FORGETTING THE REAL PURPOSE of the Christian life AND REJECTING THE ONLY WAY TO BE BORN AGAIN.

This 'born-again' subject is referred to in Alexander Hislop's The Two Babylons. According to Hislop, being born again on earth is a long-standing pagan belief.

Hislop quotes Asiatic Researchers (Vol. vii, p. 271, London, 1806) that the Hindu Brahmins boast that they are 'twice born' men.

The book quotes the Catholics' belief (from Hay, Bishop. Hay's Sincere Christian, Vol 1., p.356, Dublin, 1783) that infant baptism is to 'regenerate us by a new spiritual birth' or in other words, infant baptism is how one becomes 'born again.' Hislop quotes Prescott's Conquest of Mexico (Vol iii, pp. 339-340, London, 1843) that Catholic missionaries were shocked by the similarities of the pagan baptismal ceremonies to their own. In this pagan ceremony it was stated that the infant is 'born anew.'

Hislop seemed to feel that the concept of being born again with baptism originally was a pagan corruption of the fact that God saved Noah in an ark from the flood (many ancient civilizations recorded the flood). As Noah lived before and after the flood, he was believed to be in some sense 'born again'. The water of the flood is supposed to be a type of baptism. After some baptismal type ceremony (which did not require immersion in some cultures), the re-born individual was assured entrance to some version of paradise.

Interestingly the Roman Catholic Church has admitted that their practices of infant baptism are of an old, non-scriptural origin. Hislop quotes the 16th century Catholic theologian Jodocus Tiletanus as saying,

> We are not satisfied with that which the apostles or the Gospel do declare, but we say that, as well as before as after, there are divers matters of importance and weight accepted and received out of a doctrine which is NOWHERE SET FORTH IN WRITING. For we do blesse the water wherewith we baptize, and the oyle wherewith we annoynt; yea and besides that, him that is christened. And (I pray you) OUT OF WHAT SCRIPTURE have we learned the same? HAVE WE NOT IT OF A SECRET AND UNWRITTEN ORDINANCE? And further what scripture hath taught us to grease with oyle? Yea, I pray you, whence cometh it, that we do dype the child three times in that water? Doth it not come out of this hidden and undisclosed doctrine, which our forefathers have received closely without any curiosity, and do observe it still? (Harvet, Gentianus. Review of Epistles, PP. 19B, 20A,

London 1598, as quoted by Hislop, A. in The Two Babylons).

But what does this have to do with 'born again' from a Protestant perspective? The Catholics used to believe that babies and others who die before committing any sins will be eternally placed in a bizarre realm called 'limbo' if they have not been baptized (Pope Benedict XVI said that his church may change this). The Catholics believe you can be a terrible person, but if you have been baptized as an infant and will confess to a priest just before you die, you will go to heaven.

Certain Catholic teachings strongly emphasize the importance of ceremony (called sacraments) over living according to every word of God. From a Catholic perspective, once baptized your 'immortal soul' can access the kingdom of God. After infant baptism, all one really needs to do is confess to a priest before death and entrance into heaven is assured, no matter how one lead their life. And if you sinned after confessing to a priest and then died, after a period of purging (the length dependent upon the amount and types of sin) you then entered the kingdom of heaven.

The Protestant view is remarkably similar, except that baptism is not required of infants in most Protestant denominations. The general Protestant view appears to be that once you sin (which they usually do not clearly define; for a Biblical definition see 1 John 3:4, KJV), you must accept Jesus as your savior and then you are 'born again;' baptism is expected but does not appear to be an absolute requirement. Once you are 'born again' your 'immortal soul' is guaranteed to enter heaven upon death unless you repudiate your belief in Jesus. Sinning in any and every other way will not prevent you from entering heaven. Further repentance, though often encouraged, is not strictly necessary. In other words, when Protestants are referring to being 'born again' they are referring to a state in which one no longer needs to do to follow the laws of God in order to enter the Kingdom of God.

While it is true that eternal life is a gift of God (Romans 6:23, thus no one has an 'immortal soul') and that salvation is by the grace of God and not by our works (Ephesians 2:8), it is also true that there are

"...ungodly men, who turn the grace of our God into licentiousness" (Jude 4).

9 Do you not know that the unrighteous will not inherit the kingdom of God? Do not be deceived. Neither fornicators, nor idolaters, nor adulterers, nor homosexuals, nor sodomites, 10 nor thieves, nor covetous, nor drunkards, nor revilers, nor extortioners will inherit the kingdom of God. (1 Corinthians 6:9-10)

5 For this know, that no fornicator, unclean person, nor covetous man, who is an idolater, has any inheritance in the kingdom of Christ and God. 6 Let no one deceive you through empty words, for because of these things the wrath of God comes upon the sons of disobedience. 7 Therefore do not be partakers with them. (Ephesians 5:5-7).

Behavior matters for Christians (for more on that, see also our free online booklet: Christians: Ambassadors for the Kingdom of God, Biblical instructions on living as a Christian available at www.ccog.org).

Second, Third, and Fourth Century Writers

Even in the second century (the century just after the New Testament was written), there was at least one Christian leader that taught that we are not to be 'born again' until the resurrection. Notice what Theophilus of Antioch wrote:

> Of the Fourth Day. On the fourth day the luminaries were made; ... But the moon wanes monthly, and in a manner dies, being a type of man; then it is born again, and is crescent, for a pattern of the future resurrection (Theophilus of Antioch. To Autolycus, Book 2, Chapter XV).

An interesting thing to observe here is that the Feast of Trumpets has traditionally been the fourth biblical Holy Day and a trumpet blast is associated with Christians being born again (1 Corinthians 15:50-54).

In the third century, Hippolytus (the greatest of the early Roman Catholic theologians according to some of their scholars) understood that we are begotten by the Holy Spirit at baptism. Notice what he wrote:

> This is the Spirit that was given to the apostles in the form of fiery tongues. This is the Spirit that David sought when he said, "Create in me a clean heart, O God, and renew a right spirit within me." Of this Spirit Gabriel also spoke to the Virgin, "The Holy Ghost shall come upon thee, and the power of the Highest shall overshadow thee." By this Spirit Peter spake that blessed word, "Thou art the Christ, the Son of the living God." By this Spirit the rock of the Church was stablished. This is the Spirit, the Comforter, that is sent because of thee, that He may show thee to be the Son of God.
>
> Come then, be begotten again, O man, into the adoption of God … For he who comes down in faith to the layer of regeneration, and renounces the devil, and joins himself to Christ; who denies the enemy, and makes the confession that Christ is God; who puts off the bondage, and puts on the adoption,-- he comes up from the baptism brilliant as the sun, flashing forth the beams of righteousness, and, which is indeed the chief thing, he returns a son of God and joint-heir with Christ (Hippolytus. The Discourse on the Holy Theophany, Chapters 9,10).

Also, even in the fourth century, it was understood that Christians are first begotten, that Jesus was the first born of the dead, and that we become born again later. For even though he had other heretical ideas, Athanasius apparently understood this as he wrote:

> For God not only created them to be men, but called them to be sons, as having begotten them. For the term 'begat' is here as elsewhere expressive of a Son, as He says by the Prophet, 'I begat sons and exalted them;' and generally, when Scripture wishes to signify a son, it does so, not by the term 'created,' but undoubtedly by that of 'begat.' And this John seems to say, 'He gave to them power to become children of God, even to them that believe on His Name; which were begotten not of blood, nor of the will of the flesh, nor of the will of man, but of God.' And here too the cautious distinction is well kept up, for first he says 'become,' because they are not called sons by nature but by adoption; then he says 'were begotten,' because they too had received at any rate the name of son…He became man, that, as the Apostle has said, He who is the 'Beginning' and 'First-born from the dead, in all things might have the preeminence … He said to be 'First-born from the dead,' not that He died before us, for we had died first; but because having undergone death for us and abolished it, He was the first to rise, as man, for our sakes raising His own Body. Henceforth He having risen, we too from Him and because of Him rise in due course from the dead … He is called 'First-born among many brethren' because of the relationship of the flesh, and 'First-born from the dead,' because the resurrection of the dead is from Him and after Him … And as He is First-born among brethren and rose from the dead 'the first fruits of them that slept;' so, since it became Him 'in all things to have the preeminence (Athanasius. Discourse II Against the Arians, Chapters 59,60,61,63,64).

Thus, the idea of being begotten when converted and being born again at the resurrection is not a relatively new one among professing Christians. But unlike the idea of being born again now, it is not a concept with pre-Christian (pagan) origins.

In addition, even in more modern times, the Eastern Orthodox Church has reported:

> Frank Schaeffer…calls the standard evangelical doctrine a 'false bill of goods.' "The simplistic 'born-again' formula for instant painless 'salvation' is not only a misunderstanding, I believe it is a heresy. It contradicts the teaching of Christ in regard to the narrow, hard, ascetic, difficult way of salvation." (Clendenin D.B. ed. Eastern Orthodox Theology, 2nd ed. Baker Academic, 2003, p. 268).

Now, in the second part of this lesson (which is planned for the next edition of this magazine), we will explain more about what it really means to be born again – what it means to become a CHILD OF GOD – what the Holy Spirit actually is – and what the CONDITIONS are for receiving the Holy Spirit.

Exercise! Who Needs It?

By Patrick A. Parnell

This article was originally published in the Plain Truth magazine in December 1972

Everybody needs some form of exercise.

Why?

Because proper exercise is important to a healthy heart, efficient lungs, and a sound muscular system. Benefits include improved breathing, less excess fat, good muscle tone throughout the body, fewer tensions, and a better overall appearance. Lack of exercise contributes to obesity, atherosclerosis (a form of hardening of the arteries), and ischemic heart disease. Exercise, of course, is not a disease prevention panacea. There are too many other important factors to consider: significant overweight, whether or not you smoke, high blood pressure, what you eat. Too much exercise in fact can be detrimental to health. But moderate exercise is part of the overall picture of prevention and does profit a little.

"For bodily exercise profiteth [for a} little .. . " (I Tim. 4:8).

Those who have a sedentary type of employment especially need some form of exercise. What type of exercise you should engage in depends on your age and condition and your likes and dislikes. An older, out-of-condition person should obviously not launch into competitive sports or heavy sports activities. That would be courting danger. He or she should start out with light activities such as walking or bicycling at an easy pace, light gardening, or canoeing slowly, pitching horseshoes, playing golf, archery, and bowling and then build up to moderate activities. There are many ways to get some form of needed exercise. Ever think of using stairs instead of elevators or walking when possible, rather than riding?

Editor: Since that article came out, more and more studies have demonstrated that proper exercise improves longevity and reduces the risk for numerous diseases. Furthermore, exercise can help one feel younger and be able to be more productive in one's later years.

More FREE *Continuing Church of God* Books and Booklets
at www.ccog.org/books

The Gospel of the Kingdom of God

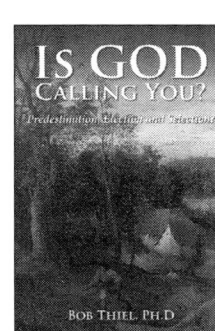
Is God Calling You?

Is God's Existence Logical?

Prayer: What Does the Bible Teach?

Youth & Singles: Q&A

Q. I am crazy about this really cute guy (or gal), but he (she) doesn't seem to know I exist. How can I get him (her) to notice me and like me?

A. The answer is that you can't. That's right, you can't get someone of the opposite sex to like you.

Don't misunderstand. This doesn't mean you are helpless to find friends of the opposite sex, or that you are doomed to a life of loneliness. There is much you can and should do if you want to have friends (Proverbs 18:24) and someday find an appropriate spouse.

In time, the person you have interest in may end up being interested in you. But you cannot force that.

You might be able to get them to notice you, but depending on them and what you do, you may turn them away from you instead of towards you.

It's not a matter of what you can get. It's a matter of what you can give.

If you are a giver, other givers will tend to be attracted to you (as will takers—so be cautious about prematurely settling for someone just because they may pay attention to you).

Q. Is it okay to wear more revealing clothes or buy an impressive car to get someone's romantic interest?

A. No.

Even if you can get someone's attention by your appearance, the car you may drive, money, smooth conversational skills, etc. that will not make them like you or truly love you.

Do you really want to marry someone that you have impressed by making yourself look seductive or by the car you drive?

If you flaunt your body or your possession, eventually the one you attract is likely to leave for one who flaunts 'better' than you.

Consider also that the Bible teaches:

22 Flee also youthful lusts; but pursue righteousness, faith, love, peace with those who call on the Lord out of a pure heart. (2 Timothy 2:22)

Christians are to have a pure heart and not pursue youthful lusts.

Those who are mainly attracted by lusts of the flesh tend to let their lusts control them and are not likely to stay with you. Those with wandering eyes, tend to continue to wander.

We are open to covering other questions that are not in our booklet as well. If you have appropriate questions that you would like answered here, you can send them to the Continuing Church of God at the address shown in the front of this magazine or send an email for consideration.

More FREE *Continuing Church of God* Books and Booklets
at www.ccog.org/books

Proof Jesus is the Messiah

The Decalogue, Christianity, and the Beast

Should You Keep God's Holy Days or Demonic Holidays?

Where Is The True Christian Church Today?

Made in the USA
Columbia, SC
11 May 2019